Branches of a House

Also by Agnieszka Studzińska

Snow Calling (2010)
What Things Are (2014)

Agnieszka Studzińska

BRANCHES OF A HOUSE

Shearsman Books

First published in the United Kingdom in 2021 by
Shearsman Books Ltd
PO Box 4239
Swindon
SN3 9FN

Shearsman Books Ltd Registered Office
30–31 St. James Place, Mangotsfield, Bristol BS16 9JB
(this address not for correspondence)

www.shearsman.com

ISBN 978-1-84861-777-3

CONTENTS

Part I

Part II

Part III

for my mother
Alicja

Part I

Ne rien dire, ne rien taire. Écrire cela. Tomber. Comme le météore. Être seul à oublier comment la nuit se déchire…

To say nothing, to allow everything to be said. To write that. To fall. Like a shooting star. To be the only one who forgets how the night is torn apart…

—Jacques Dupin

Foundations

…Now when I build, I shall begin
With the smoke from the chimney.
                    Leopold Staff

With the smoke from the chimney

With hail stones and snow

With crumpled rain

With breath in quivering air

With a falling of soot

With dew from a working field

With winter in fog

With voices of distance

With shapes in the margins

With language belonging elsewhere

With shadows dismantled

With the haunting of walls

With the brume of writing

With ink inhabiting skin

Whose hands shape these structures?

Whose architecture or bones?

Whose history in the hem of skirts

In the pockets of brickwork?

Architecture

lines \ annex & rive \ bracket \ paper landscapes & \ lines of humanity \ clayed & constructed \ called upon \ materials of tenure & term \ what is this space if not us? \ configured nests & soft symmetries \ bodies in lovemaking \ irregular forms of sensuality \ criss-crossing conceptions \ solidity & our names \ pencilled identities \ you touch this groundwork \ draw my lineation \ feel the edges like a rough cut \ erase me \ insert me back\ erase me again \ in lust & downfall & draughtsmanship \ we loose our footing \ in these skin-stone buildings \ we build from ourselves\ we are invisible lines of sculpture & detail \ thresholds in need of safety \ we hammer & knock \ secure flesh & façades in our tentative versions \ align blood with the grind of history \ our undeclared kisses \ blown apart \

Brick

Irregular palettes of colour – stung yellow, mustard brown, buried shades – off white, umber lining scabrous to the soft fingers of a child who traces its exterior as he learns to walk in a house. It is as if the brick moves through him or we through the brick, the house changing in registers of light. Far away, another house rehearses ghost language & dance, interprets the seasons of snow spoken winters, spring shadowed with unsent letters, summers sated with summer rain & autumn from its fleeting blush. There are bricks wherever we look & fallen branches & families re-writing their version of what they were told. There are ghost houses in every village & houses in every ghost as it enters through an open window of that distant dwelling while you bury yourself deeper inside it. You too move through these bricks, the blue wind cooling your almost blue face while you listen to conversations cobwebbed in unlikely corners. In sleep you scan all the occupations & childhoods & weddings, perceive bodies that once lived inside you, smell their small hands stretching towards futures, in & away from this structure. You welcome these waxy flashes, loneliness writes its own, on these walls where photographs hang flattened by daylight & error. You welcome their supple illusions, the wisp & sail of their flux, in which you are spun & swaddled & taken back to where you began. The wind in petal, rising ash, & the brick now, coated by cheap paint, floorboards tiled, stories cloaked in this notebook of home, as we ghost linger in these irregular palettes of colour, stung yellow, mustard brown, buried shades – breath building bricks in preparation for a house to be that house again –

Attic

My origin is a linguistic surface like a decorated wall
Mei Mei Berssenbrugge

The cutting of the white rose bush is sent by post, roots like a spider's cuticular hairs navigating a way in this sensory field of plant, source, descent. Upstairs, the builders pull apart the attic. Brick from wall, joint from hinge, screw from wood, substance from structure. The morning mislaid in segments, glimmer, & dust, like a waking dream from a precipice I refuse to jump. Downstairs, sounds lean on interruptions, light unstable in these lines of keeping & remove. What is the drift of silence? Where is the wilful murmur of our origins? I ask M. the next day. Outside, the rose remains in a bucket. Roots absorb all the cold water. Inside, the noise of things falling in their inconsistent, shattered way lament, as they stake themselves to our forms where definitions hedge the living we once inhabited.

Body House

after *House of Self*—Alice Notley

There I go
in her voice I find
what's missing
& drift in & out
                    of self
find it hard
all this
            going back
to house   my body
house again   my body
body house –
another wall & room
                    doors open
the smell of ghosts
                on my body
& traces of sapling & oak
young shoulders
& grandmother observing
saying
you really are a woman now
at 19   I was
            yet still a child
in that *child house* –
how difficult
to have missed my growing
nothing
can bring that back
not this body
standing before her
the body in the house
I left
the body in the house
I came back to –

my body house in sunder
just her & I
closing in
like trees in woods
bringing two bodies
together
two women
inside the house
        of their bodies
& I
hover
in this coppice of house
all blood, cortex & bark
& brush the back
        of our necks
pull this breeze
        between branches
& begin moving away
                again
always moving
& because of her
I am
I say
I am
Writing this. I write like this.

Area

1

Measurements and weights of this planet are written in beautiful equations.

Earth's mass reads like this:
$M_\oplus = 5.9722 \times 10^{24}$ kg

Earth's weight, a suitcase of numbers unfolding in their invisibility.

Ungraspable, these remote lines of formulae like ancestry, this mathematics.

Earth's prevailing blue pulls you down as you sink in its domesticity.

I want to calculate the space of diaspora, that delicate body.

She asks what *I* means for you? She wants to be that direct.

Her surname has been hidden, only now swells to a surface.

Did you have to change your name? She asks.

Trees recumbent in their sculptural volume of wood, waste and undoing.

A boy climbs the branches of a sycamore with his bow and arrow in position.

2

Perception draws itself into shapes that look like solid structures.

I watch benchmarks on walls and mirrors disappearing.

The map of my body house folded in an envelope.

I fishtail in the space of that photograph. We become inseparable.

I want to scope sex in this keeping of us like boxes.

I envy the gaze of that animal when it looks beyond you.

Shoes in hallways in exact compositions of distance and place.

I re-learn the circuit of childhood through his gestures.

I need to be objective about the missing.

This area between us – beryl and breeding, longs to remain.

This is our itinerary: fields, apples, figurines, absence.

Spring

The magpie hops down from the arms of a fig tree stopping mid branch in scrutiny of the blackbird's nestling in the curtain length of clematis sprawling against the garage wall. There is no glint to capture his attention as he jumps down further listening to the coiled calls of the blackbird circling her unmade home. From a distance my husband waters plants – though it has rained the night before – quickly dipping the can into the rain-filled barrel. The blackbird, the magpie & the husband move through the sun's pallid signature – a suggestion of permanency arrested in thickets of light. The neighbour has started a bonfire & the smoke of dead things & wood cling to clothes, feathers & seep into frond, corkscrew through the branches of a fig tree like a stairwell leading to the cellar brimming with furnishings concealed from our view.

Summer

Perhaps it was here, but we missed it, clammed in our shell houses – individuality & sickness in ocean waves warped all our intentions under flowering beds of bacillus, upon a world in virulent green. Silted, costumed, reversed. We do not know what to make of this – this hitherto – this beforehand – this attending – this destruction to make body & landscape again. We are molluscs deep in telluric tide, incalculable motes in the splendour of heat. We are far from the home we have built & yet we are right here – like solitude in rods of salvia, in the sphere of peony, in the thorns of blackberry & bramble, our walled gardens & thought in majestic shades of austerity, black purple & white. Perhaps this default in closeness & touch, this lack of resemblance, a scalloped season resigned, is our drill & practice in this late adjusting to now.

Autumn

Driftwood white of sky, barely touching the stratagem
of fallen leaves, the pother of reds & oranges, undersides
folding, unanswerable, unrequited – I step on their torment,
a network of rusted blades & measureless tales – I walk to
unsettle their orderless piles & then in the woods relent,
forage every stipule, every verb, every crossroad of vacillant
colour – I drape among branches, hear bicycle wheels flank
tracks, shapeless sounds of girls giggle, call out their scent
to nameless boys & the awkward beauty of their shouting
shedding itself in that first kiss against the ridges of bark,
hands blinded by breath, scale to scale in mimicry of nature.
We are meshed in this patina of collapsed desire & desire
budding, tremor of leaf-play, the skein of geese in a shrilled
chorus of flight – underfoot the tips of a crocus splintered.

Winter

It could be September again. *Clement* is how the presenter describes the day. I say *Changed*. Nothing is as expected. Even the berries from the holly tree discarded their red small spectres months ago. This gravelled path is a riverbed for all that swims in these dumped and pimpled waters. Forever uncertain in how it could shoulder or displace the bloodshed, the berries, the wasting of intelligent minds. The fog comes easily the following day. As does TV news. Your own speculations. The earth crawling in its own shadow of corruption or democracy, cells dividing into tiny abstractions of uneven skin & winter faltering in these frail, plastic temperatures. Too hot. Too cold elsewhere. Too young. What gift of polar bear, arctic fox, is left under our trees at night? What rising of light will dapple our shelters, record our breaking with this luminous apple?

Homegrown

Faint snow-scaled winter air

                                        she held the coffee

scooped the dimpled film

                                        of milk in her mouth

froth dissolved snowflakes

                                        on the peak of speech

fell on chalked dermis

                                        the areola of a chocolate heart

spreading as she spoke of diagnosis

                                        the bitter gloss sown in her throat –

winter roofed

                                        the open surfaces of up-turned ground

roots spinning like silk worms

                                        in their execution for the cocoon

that eventually kills them.

Stół

This table of wetlands & fields

       of carp   borsch   pierogi

of birch forests   their boned dignity   pastures of

tea stains   in oil cloth   & solitary birds in shrubs

         of material

    the sky white   &   almost painless –

I walk this table empty   of what you cook

& what you say   in a language rendered

       & crumbled

on my tongue   &   vanishing –

a stirring of spoons   forks digging

    the scrape of this cutlery

    widening our rivers   & salted lakes

    rings of tomatoes & family codes

in a marsh of sound   as we swallow matter & matriarchy

     & sugared blackberries

drink village wars –   homemade struggles

lace themselves in napkins

like small tapestries of   woven food & women & wood

     &   their men in territories

far from

       our hunger.

Blue

Blue is a slipped silence. A silence speaking. A figure visible then vanished. A slant in perception. Contradictory. Indifferent. A body in water. The water of scattered light. The turquoise of toxins. This lake. Detained. Surfacing from the pretext. A body inside another body. The stammer of pleasure. Essence, called love or soul. Ink on skin. Blue is the branded. Brushed history. Apology. An unfurling mind. Curfews of church bells. Mountains laced with footprints. Oil on fingernails. Oil on weapons. Demolished homes. Bruised walls. Bricks. Air between language and implication. Flickering minutes of dawn. Ghosts in a house. The left behind. Their confession. The bluebell fence of borderlines and beatings. A child's shout from the camp. Blue is their tongue. Their mother. Turning heads. Error. The dinghy mottling the sea with frigid weight. Swimming. Caged water. Blue is the silk of a blouse. Blue is the waiting. Blue is what remains.

Voice

A voice lies buried in a river driving
its long skeletal frame across spliced
boundaries hidden in the vellum
of summer, deep in this tissue &
crust, under the pious fires of a city
standing half full of visible darkness
or light or neither – this place
a papier-mâché model collapsing
into plated grey of printed walls
frescoes bulleted, dappled with blood
& graffiti – voice crawls in the
pinholes & dust of their standing.
Maybe voice is our grit in the low
hum of a mid afternoon adapting,
the broken harmonica in rubble.
Voice wraps this rutted earth in chords
& layers of other inaudible voices
the scintilla of their invisible sound,
tongues curling in many attempts.
Once it smelt of cooking oil, bread,
crushed dates, white jasmine,
the blossom of anguish and apples,
the flannelled orange of your pyjamas.

Spaces

You walk to the hotel from the train station. The evening footsteps behind you. Carrying one small bag on your right shoulder, you observe the unfamiliar buildings. You turn left. Then left again. You hear someone singing. The evening drains the light from your skin. You find the hotel tucked away in a back street. It spines awkwardly. Your room is on the 8th floor. You take the lift avoiding the mirror. The strap of the bag deepening. In the corridor, you hear a group of men underlining words in a language you don't understand. A baby moans elsewhere. On the third attempt you open the door. You sit on the bed and observe the walls and ceiling. Outside someone shouts 'Fuck you - you took that fucking kiss, you can do what the fuck you want.' You move towards the window. You discover there is no view, just a narrow space between one building and another. The geometry of this distance is inscribed on you like a birthmark. You touch it with your fingers on the window. Your body is glass. You hear the sky darkening into its own tumescent kingdom. You return to the bed. You listen. There are voices composing operas. You think of the run in the park last week. You hear again, 'You took that fucking kiss.' But you know the man is not there. You think of your father. You think of houses inside other houses. You stand up. Someone else stands up with you. The room departs in the abstract shapes of anonymity, pushing.

Doorway

Bad luck, she says as she moves beyond the frame, and their kiss is free from adversity, the earth's black insolvable algebra. *And now before the door I dared not enter*, Emily writes as she lingers outside. Which is where they stand, listening to the doorbell announcing their arrival. Pillar-box red, army green, weathered yellow, wood peeping through. The dog's bark is a warning. Often, she walks into doors, pretending it doesn't hurt. Whispers widen into arguments. Doors are marked with names. There is a tight-lipped knock. The afternoon is potholed with rain. He watches films where doors flap like bird wings. They bulldoze the door with their boots and find a game of dominoes scattered on the table, black tea and biscuits beside the tiles. In the painting, the rectangular shapes resemble openings - there is no subject in this canvas, just the symmetry of paint. Someone has betrayed us. The bookcase is not really a bookcase. The wallpaper is wrinkled. Their backs are against the door of the house. *Can we read a door in the same way we read a wall?* he asks in a lecture on a Friday morning. He dusts off the pastry from a croissant settled on the breastbone of his suit. They are squeezing each other's hands in comfort. She pretends she can't hear. They want to go back. Her suitcase contains no clothes just letters from him, she leaves it, abandoned. In summer, the back door opens to the sea as salt powders the house. The heat confesses. Sea waves unlock shells, rift their posterity.

Flamingo

She notes the ink markings on his arms
his uncaged   elegance
                    against the shudder of a train
the marl of back roads, sheets of grass
a succession of houses
            that appear before him & vanish
inside her –   their worlds narrowing – inside
            the body of this train
his skin speaks
& she is all flamingo
standing in the water   spreading her wings
            her neck twisting into
                    an ampersand connecting
all that is flesh with feathers
            as the train
crowded with water
                    thick with algae
advances through
a landscape of latches, hinges, keyholes,
this wild life
in which we are forever
susceptible
scored   mislaid.

Still Life with Fruit, Bird Nest and Broken Eggs

after George Forster

Here

the nest is almost perfect –
     & the fruit scratched
rests uneasily –
     & if there
     appears an order
in which these objects are arranged
or chosen
     away from their habitat
       then
it is beyond   my learning
in this alloy of morning
     & interruption
by your shout from the kitchen
to *come quick*
as you watch
a fallen fledgling
struggle under the tree.
It is useless
     I think
as we near its swollen body
still fighting
for whatever is left
     as if our approach
disrupts
the mahogany-depth of a backdrop
unbinding
      injury & ruin –
& we try to rebuild
    in a leaf-filled shoe box
hear the clatter

of mother bird's wings –
       & mine
on your growing body
       thrash also
in desperation for things
       to remain the same
between
the walls of twigs
       & lichen
a garden
       & the second fledgling
       following
this patterned line of failure
       while we wait
helplessly
our attempts
       obscured
       as if the light had drawn
its own preserve of broken
       & yellow
       confidence emptying –
it shapes
       our composition &
collapses in the folds of our speech –

Permanence

But you said you wouldn't he repeated. *I never said I wouldn't,* she replied. *You said you would try.* His voice flat between the white sheets and the constellation of their vernacular, meteoric, morning pressed on his lips in a yellow shiver. *You promised.* She focused on the open window, revealing a contour of rooftops against the city's urban undertones, tree tops folded like centuries invisible to their own waking & the blue bottle airborne in the left-hand corner of the frame; the drone of its flight vibrating in the fastened stillness of their ground and entering. She observed the finish of its metallic body, as it moved towards them. In the background, voices on the radio held barrage and shelling, the sky dismembered. She switched it off. *Why did you do that?* a voice asked. Her eye followed the blue bottle handwriting the air as it paused from one sentence to another on the periphery of the room. She heard him roll the newspaper & tiptoe in the direction of a cupboard, *I am gonna kill the dirty bastard,* he whispered. *Leave it,* she heard herself reply, rising out of bed & stepping out of his shadow. She knew that flies did not build nests & their eggs hatched in rotting matter, understood how despised their species. She watched them both in the desolate spaces of a room, the pale cries of newborns settling on this single stalk of morning breeze as she headed for the window to catch this soft current.

This Could All Be

Destroyed. Damaged. Obliterated.

I hear such words on TV performing their customs in wildfires, riots & protests.

Rain varnishes windows, surfaces of nature's secrets & our faces returning.

The spelling list includes the word: *erosion* in its practice of the suffix *-sion;* as in invasion.

Evidence suggests an Iranian missile brought down a Ukrainian passenger plane.

The air is a nest for bacteria & bodies multiply in need to be re-housed.

Polluted whispers & mothers of missing children scan the littered streets.

The neighbour artist paints with her abstract language. *I want to experiment with how paint sounds*, she says.

I look at the red square in her sketchbook & depict a red landscape.

I hear it in them – dead under a bus or buying fruit at a market.

I promise to remember the small things.

Rain trapped inside the human body.

I hear it in you.

In her sketchbook, she writes, *are some holes too big to fix?*

The rain folds air in its wings, flaps the afternoon into chaos.

I made these disrupted drawings, she says.

I made these disrupted words to mean something to you.

I consider how earth was formed as he talks about the power of stardust in Pokémon.

There are celebrations of a new decade or the killing of a state leader.

I read: *blinded by chemical dust* in her eyes.

Promises. Promises. Promises.

Pencil markings of rupture strikethrough her notebook.

I hear it in you.

She titles her work, *The Beauty of Holes.* What is the deepest hole in the world? I ask.   -

There are layers of time in the layers of paint she applies to the canvas.

There are layers of sentences in the clothes I wear, phrases settled in cotton.

The future imperfect. Star trek.

A continuous tense like the rigorous rain shedding her skin for the next generation.

I hear it in you.

Cityscapes

The family are wild flowers on the roadside verge.

Sleep belongs to the living in a village collapsed with hunger.

A plaza of people are shadowed in broken café windows.

The city slides – revealing empty swallow nests, shaven earth.

Out of the crooked timber of humanity, no straight thing was ever made, writes Kant.

Streets hold the footfall of new generations splintered in the skins of the old.

Each building deepens in a parallelogram of wind. *Where are you?*

A landscape disfigured by your perception of beauty.

Who is the woman heading towards you, avoiding your glare?

You walk in spaces vacated by others and occupied with their spent.

The confidence of this view breaks in the sighs of a fire.

Sit here on the pavement and detail the birds reconstructing the sky.

And the city replies to your childhood with drab light.

A family of ghosts in the hospitality of house and estrangement.

Hide in this city and listen to the labour of birdcalls in distant nests.

Stories hang in small balconies among laundry and flower-pots.

A city startled and shifting in a misreading of place.

Stay here and listen to *that something not being said is speaking.*

Notes Towards a Poem

after Joseph Conrad, *Heart of Darkness*

1. This morning an orchestra of cicadas cluster in small olive trees, veiling from summer wind. Their punctual song maps the Aegean air. We listen to the measures of nature, the cyclical accents of a language unlacing, the world camouflaged with this heat.

2. *And at last, in its curved and imperceptible fall, the sun sank low and from glowing white changed to a dull red without rays and without heart, as if about to go out suddenly, stricken to death by the touch of that gloom brooding over a crowd of men* (Conrad: 2015: 4).

3. Suddenly, the cicadas stop on cue. The backbone of this landscape eases. I smell the whispered trail of fire as our children nosedive in the swimming pool. Suddenly, somewhere boys and girls their age stop on cue. Taken to the markets and sold for a healthy price.

4. *They were conquerors and for that you want only brute force – nothing to boast of when you have it, since your strength is just an accident arising from the weakness of others. They grabbed what they could get for the sake of what was to be got* (Conrad: 2015:7).

5. The African migrants imprisoned in Libya, stretch their limbs through bars like off shoots of a dead tree in the sheath of sun. The broken promise of money is white hot and burning.

6. *But I couldn't. I could not tell her. It would have been too dark – too dark altogether* (Conrad: 2015: 84).

7. In 2016, more than 180,000 migrants crossed from Libya to Italy. According to the UN, almost 26,000 of these were children, most of them unaccompanied.[1]

---

[1] http://www.bbc.co.uk/news/world-africa

8. *I wanted to cross the sea, look for work, earn a bit of money, help my five brothers* reads the sentence. *They would flog my head, my hand, my bum,*[2] reads another.

9. In bed, our children shawl their bodies between thin cotton sheets. The butterfly kiss of the eyelash flutters in sleep. I think of adults turning into children and children into adults. Sleep comes cautiously.

10. *They would let us phone our people once a day*, he said. *They would whip us while we were on the call so our families would get the message. We would beg them to send us money.*[3]

11. We jump off small rocks rounding a bay and swim together to the shore. The sea bluffing in turquoise. The sky meets it seamlessly.

12. *Very well; I hear; I admit, but I have a voice too, and for good or evil mine is the speech that cannot be silenced* (Conrad: 2015: 39).

13. The economic migrant and the apparition of a future.

14. *I like to read about the dead people*, my daughter tells me as she explains why history is her favourite subject.

15. After the fire had ransacked the land behind our villa, we watched the hawks as they swooped closer to the ground still looking for prey.

16. *The foreigner lives within us: he is the hidden face of our identity...?"* writes Kristeva.[4]

17. The cicadas cower with sheen like jewelled broaches on the collar of a coat.

18. The sweetness of fresh orange juice disguises what we are saying.

---

[2] http://www.bbc.co.uk/news/world-africa
[3] http://www.bbc.co.uk/news/world-africa
4 Kristeva Juliya, *Strangers to Ourselves* (trans Leon S. Roudiez), Columbia University Press, New York, 1991.

19. ...*It is impossible to convey the life-sensation of any given epoch of ones existence – that which makes truth, its meaning – its subtle and penetrating essence. It is impossible. We live, as we dream – alone.* (Conrad: 2015: 29)

20. I think of the water heartbroken with darkness, pushing down as far as it can reach. How in its endless cycle of ablution, it cannot cleanse the taste of salt from itself, from those who enter its household.

An essay on *The Dragon and the Invisible Creatures*

The houses that were lost forever… insist in us in order to live again.
—Gaston Bachelard

An introduction is always rewritten. The *I* returns to the beginning having travelled through the *country of words*.[5] Beginnings are conjectural. The concept of unity – that of a beginning, middle and end is based on the idea that each part depends upon the other. Each portion pivotal to make whole. But what if your beginnings are indiscernible? What then of wholeness?

Today has turned. The air folded down to coldness. Salt migrates along the pavement in the anticipation of snow. But there will be no snow. No real snow anyway – just a ghostliness in its disappearing as it pretends to fall. So close, so near to snow. Home becomes yours in the residual of snow that never fell.

I leave the house with coffee, drink its habit and think about my six-year old son who last night followed me up to the attic. *I want to write a story on your computer in posh writing,* he said (he wanted to use italics). And if italics emphasise a point, if they highlight importance, then –

One day there was a dragon. He said to his mummy and daddy "why do we have to go out?" We are just going out for a little bit said his mummy. "How long?" asked the dragon. "Not long- about 15 minutes" replied his mummy. "That's long in my world." So in the end they went out for dinner. Some minutes later some little small creatures appeared in the shadows. They looked in the bins. And started throwing cardboard, cans, cat food and plastic bottles. "What was that" said the dragon? How many creatures were there? There were about 81 of them. The creatures have changed into foxes.

I do not correct his punctuation yet help him when he asks to spell *appeared* and *creatures*. I am curious about the creatures in the shadows

---

[5] Sellers Susan: (ed) *The Hélène Cixous Reader*. Routledge: London and New York: 1994: "At a certain moment when one loses everything, whether that means a being or a country, language becomes the country of words." xxvii

and his unintentional metaphysical questions – Is change *really* possible? What is time? Why are we leaving? Although the last question is not metaphysical, it's a question about possibilities.

The self-possession of a house in the shadows of September. On the balcony of the house, a girl and her grandparents pose for a photograph. From below, the photographer captures what has already left. In this leaving, the girl folds the house in its paper, hides it inside the pocket of her jacket.

In the attic your father's ashes rest in a wooden box waiting for his wife. *I've had a good life*, she said as if her presence negated the space in which she lives.

In the kitchen I am cooking dinner, listening to a mother on the radio, *at least in heaven there's food*, she tells the world, whilst waiting for her child to die, *heaven will be our new home*, she whispers between the gunfire and the metal clanks of empty pots.

I start the engine of the car and the city accelerates through the space of where I live now. The palimpsest of houses forms a fog of homes in wintered light. They are somehow absent from their own architecture. Buildings in which home is made and unmade. *A strange house contained in my voice.* [6]

Early history survives on fragments. Writings ghosted with voices.

us, you, him, she, they, them   marks on a page

on territories   *don't be afraid*

Fragments, *…unfinished separations, their insufficiency, the disappointment at work in them is their aimless drift…neither unifiable nor consistent, they accommodate a certain array of marks…"*[7] Surely, we are all a series of unfinished separations?

---

[6] Seghers Pierre: *Le Domaine Public*: Editions Lucien Parizeau: 1946: 79
[7] Blanchot Maurice: *The Writing of the Disaster* (trans Ann Smock): University of Nebraska: Lincoln, NE and London: 1995

My son is rooted in this language, in his construction of place and the *One Day* of a story. This unfinished story like all stories – even finished ones.

I notice the determined, mantling of the Japanese Anemone in December. I read on a website how difficult it is to eradicate this flower, how persistent and invasive their kind, how deep their rhizome spreads.

Home is the return to where distance did not yet count.[8] I think I know what this means but I am not certain. In the place of the undefined meaning becomes yours.

If there *was* a conclusion, I would summarise *here*.

---

[8] Berger John: *and our faces, my heart, brief as photos*: Bloomsbury: 2005: 91

Port

"One ship is very much like another and the sea is always the same..."
—Joseph Conrad

In May unsullied clouds haul across a sky dotted with seabirds. I point towards them. My children eat their snacks staring at the wry, moss-grey waters of the Thames. It stretches & turns as if a colony of human hands were pulling it out of its skin – poached identities flicker on the water's rim as the sun anchors in the ditches of marshland. We are here on this coastal path against the shadows of a town redundant. Ghostly diligence folds in disused buildings. The lines of the river scribble the language of her dark intentions. Late afternoon approaches. I point to the map & ask if we are to head further. The children say no. I point in the direction of Tilbury docks, past the pylons, cranes, the wind turbines scything the air for energy, a tableaux of industry in which we are the only humans. I point to the map & show them the docks. It looks like a bent fork, my son replies. Gulls above fly like undelivered parcels. Their weight dents the sky as they cargo inside its grip. They are migratory I say. My daughter asks what this means. To travel from one country or a climate to another, fish & animals do this I reply. We are animals my son says & I nod, yes, people too, pointing to their sweet wrappers held in their hands like tickets. I google gulls. The herring gull appears on the page. The sentence, *seabirds have always proven elusive subjects to study*, glares on the screen. I am surprised at how many species there are & how difficult it is to identify them. They are described on one site as intelligent & adaptable. I think of the latter, the skill & perseverance of this undertaking. To re-adjust. Are you listening? I look up. We are hungry the children announce. I point to the docks again. Look at the fork. It is a port on the river Thames, it's very old I say & try to count from 1886. A port is, I begin, a place of arrival & departure. I try to explain words like employment, freight, struggle & shipment, how the things we like or use are transported & there are these boxes on board these ships called containers & inside them – they heard the banging, the dehydrated screaming of children & women, 35 voices squashed in their own desperation inside this steel- promise for something better. And no, *one ship is not very much like another.* This one imported 1 dead man, 8 men remained, 8 women & 13 children between 1 & 12. I am trying not to imagine those children, the smell of fear, or want even, not imagine what happened before or after or during this journey, their skins encased, waiting to be eaten. Imagine not if they were sent back to their country or the outcome of the criminal investigation or how unequal & arbitrary living becomes – just like last week, stopping at the red light in my car, I saw a woman squatting against a shop wall. I tried not to look but we seized the other in the lacework of passing. I tried not to imagine the things she had lost, now wavering between the fog of exhaust fumes, these cars & and us. I thought of the man on the You Tube video filming the back of a lorry in his own lorry near Calais. How the men come out from nowhere, how they thumped on the door, how they managed to open the back, how the man filming in the lorry was tutting, how the man filming in the lorry ignored the hand-blows on his own door as he shouted, *get a passport.* I tried not to imagine what was inside his head. I tried not to imagine this urgent, frantic, possibility of a leaving, of resigning identity, of the cool compliance of the sea shouldering bodies, my own mothering body now notched like the imperfect perfect apples I eat as if tasting myself through their flushed-red, yellow-green peel, packaged in plastic on which reads: *wonky apples.* I eat their wonkinesss. I recycle the wrapping – what of protection I think & convenience & price & the plastic that blossoms in the urban loam, & the plastic ducks & toys bobbing out to sea. But of this damage you know already, this world signified, in sign, pointing to itself or elsewhere, beyond culture, to a place of no language or light in *the black bank of cloud,* where hearts indeed grow darker, the earth smaller & the ocean crowded with impermeable secrets. In pointing to the fork, I pause & say nothing of all this. I change route. Shall we take the ferry across? Like fisherman, sea captains, pirates, stowaways, following the river as it opens to the sea.

Biography of *H*

H stands like an intimation of a figure emerging   walls
                    in a palette of fog
doors stripped   marked with initials & woodworm   ajar
        &   inviting itself to acknowledge the harvest
      an appearance in a poise of quiet & susurration
                like the entering of two minds in the body of language
      outside   above this horizon   cars & horse-carts pass
forest fires erupt   poppy fields flower small hands & tiny animals
    birds   line pylon wires   their twines of speech style
          an afternoon of nesting   or   seeking

—

in other small corners   a little girl sits in a house   &
       in that house   her father's death   has not yet happened
  but his shape filters the breadth   of that place   as mice
      scurry   under wild grasses of floor   to cavities
  &   lapses in ground   beckoning   our shadowed
lives in brick   in bark   &   cave of leaf   in water
       in its own alluring migration   this openwork trembles
in her knowledge   &   the landscape staggers   with burden
     in pulse   sequence   in microscopic particles
         of what love
        &   looking after   determines

Cave

This morning I climb deeper
into the light's yellow meadow
under the grain of this substance
inside its wild flowering of logic
a sprawling of shadows
on walls or a language
in shadow in a morning
of rain after rain
                     & there I am
in my own cave
pig deer – bovine – ancient hands
mulberry ink – these spears –
scribbles of existence
in the rifts of plaster & stone
& the mind's weathering rock.
I seep through cowslip beauty
to a leaf on the branch of a flower
a mask on the stem of a tree
a world in disorder
my own sex somewhere
in this demise –
What rests in these imperfections?
in simple marks of baring
of who we were & what we saw
& how we are to become?
What do I recognise?
What head of a bird or face of a daughter?
Which objects echo such truths?
rebounding their dark
from our glance.

Part II

It is so difficult to find the beginning. Or better:
it is difficult to begin at the beginning. And try
not to go further back.
                    — Wittgenstein, *On Certainty*

Branches of a House

I

She packs lightly travels light
light –
closed in her mouth like a clump of smoke

spilling away

parting from places in her small history
light –

as in   all the things she hadn't taken
where hidden inside her

or light   as in
blind panic
                the way a person might flee
from remembering –

Memory is a house on fire
                in the bones of brick
in possession of her.

II

It is the end of a stretched autumn.

Through the blue skinless light
                she follows a mapped landscape –
the hessian yellow of earth – the dense green tips
                                of slanted shelter.
An unlevelled sky opens

to a flowering of buildings and rain as the airplane descends.

Between reading and watching
                              she closes her eyes
and counts backwards.

III

They sit in the porch overlooking that garden, the tidiness unfamiliar.

The gooseberry bush is a shadow apprehending not occasion but loss.

A girl loops her childhood on the branches of a walnut tree.

The grandmother prays, sleeps, prays and smiles at the apparition.

He lights a cigarette. They speak between the rings of smoke.

The birds billow, perfecting their unyielding haunted dance.

The house breathes her out. She breathes you back in.

They speak in silence, the blue shadows of breath misspell *home*.

A grandmother in measures of light that renders her invisible.

Windows shudder to the shape-shifting bodies of starlings.

Of arrival –   beyond us –   a soft disappearance –

                                        if a memory.

IV

Children struggle to survive sub-zero temperatures in Belgrade. Frostbite like leeches. It is 2016. The newspaper reports that he is from Afghanistan. It could be a different year. A different country or child. He sleeps in an old train station on the pillow of the platform. *My school was destroyed and my home too,* he says. The slogan *Kosovo in Serbia* is painted on the carriage of a train. The wars are old now – all of them – even the new ones. Elsewhere, a hospital tunnelled underground in a secret location – 12 doctors – 1,000 patients and swallows of ammunition swoop the carcass of a sky. It does not stop. Not here. Voices confirm – *we will defend every inch of our territory.* Think daisy chains. Think districts and neighbourhoods. What of their smell? What of their people? Or the woman who is a child returning? What of her country buried under paper and smoke?

V

A city was rebuilt, working from photographs, drawings, memory.
Ask – whose memory, drawings, photographs?
Ask – What *things we have forgotten are housed*?

VI

Crows are strung between branches
                    autumn pierces their blackness –
a world written with raindrops
                    and language vanishing even as it emerges

If a thought then this –
                    darker than sepia
sequestered
            worn   gnarled like a wishbone:

That night she let you enter her home and the rain

        washed them away with their secret.

Nights fold into one another – as do homes and rain and secrets.

A century ago, a battlefield of crows –
                    a woman leaves a mother behind.

VII

This is not what you remember
if a memory
this not what you knew but it has drawn you as you speak
if a memory
this is not visible
if a memory
this is not your voice in the woods with the trills of birdsong
if a memory
this is not the house where insects circle the smoke of a candle
if a memory
this is not the house but it stood *here*
if a memory
this is not why you lost faith in humanity
if a memory
this is not the umbrella of *caesium* cloud arresting daybreak
if a memory
this is not you parading naked before them
if a memory
or kneeling all night on all fours, holding up bricks
if a memory
this is not the doorstep you sat on shelling photographs
if a memory
this is not a bale of newsprint yellowing in distorted facts
if a memory
this is not your *need*
if a memory
this is not you returning to the open disguise of rain
if a memory –

Conversations

The language of awaiting – perhaps it is silent, but it does not separate speaking and silence; it makes of silence already a kind of speaking; already it says in silence the speaking that silence is
                    —*Maurice Blanchot*

It starts with a silence

then a shattered gaze
                    into ceilings

                    out of windows
                                   and finally

the mother inside of her speaking
                                   of the mother outside

                    and the mother of –
— *I am angry*

                                   [Silence is a voice learning to listen]

— Her emotions are not your emotions, she says

— *I dreamt that my father had three other children*

— How did that make you feel?

— *Cheated*

[The vulpine morning slides away
                    · the opal of its gait quickening]

— *I am not good at staying with things*

— Why not?

— *I don't know. I once dreamt in Polish, it was the only time*

— Tell me a word in Polish

— *Babcia*

— What does *Babcia* mean?

— *Grandmother*

— Tell me about your grandmother?

— *I washed her feet once. I put slices of fresh lemon in the bowl of water. I wanted her feet ready for dancing.*

> [Piano keys distil from a radio – globules of scores pattern the kitchen's woodwork – bird voices – bird feet – raindrops dance against sealed windows– generations gently chalked in annotations of melody]

— Are we talking about your mother or your daughter?

— *I don't know*

— Or perhaps you are speaking of someone else?

— *Who?*

— That's not for me to answer

> [The spoon is gone – the spoon is here – the mother is gone – the mother is here]

— Can you try to answer that? she replies

— *I've been thinking about what I could say tonight?*

— And what do you think?

— *I repeat myself?*

— And?

— *I've been thinking about this process*

— Ok

— *And how we hold things back*

— You?

— *Yes, my mother too.*

[The accent of the pencil – sketches snow – modulation of snow muffled in language – snowstorms inside skin – snow language clustered in a throat hardening]

— Explain what you hear?

— *I want to start at the beginning*

— What does that mean?

— *I am finding it difficult to remember*

— Remember what?

— *The beginning*

— It's ok, you don't have to try to remember

— *But isn't that why I am here?*

> [Brick upon brick – voices in brick resounding. Shapes rousing in hallways – a mural of shadows moving beyond the house]

— The shadows, she says, let's start with the shadows.

— *When she came back, she cut my hair*

— Why do you think that happened?

— *An assertion of power*

— Over what?

— *I don't know*

— How long was she away for?

— *I don't know*

— Can you tell me more?

— *No.*

> [Draw a house in a basin of moonlight – draw the child – now draw the house a child might draw – where does it stand on a page?]

— *He didn't tell me she died.*

— Was he trying to protect you?

— *He denied me*

— And now you are?

— *Angry*

— Because he didn't' tell you?

— *Yes*

— Would you feel comfortable saying this to him?

— *No*

— Do you think he needed you not to be there?

— *I've never been there*

— And that's a problem?

— *I just find it difficult*

— You feel betrayed?

— *I feel invisible. I feel that he didn't listen*

— Listen?

[A trumpet wraps silence against
thin houses – piano notes in mouths
instead of speech – a porcelain
dance in whitened rooms – portraits
glimmer in windows —likeness
slackening as trembling hands close
them shut]

— *I think I'd like to stop*

— Why?

— *I am tired of talking*

— Is that what you think?

— *It's how I feel?*

— But what do you think?

— *That I would like to write a letter*

— And will you?

— *No*

> [In an orchard starved of fruit – bodies
> trickle in gunfire – photographs languish
> in pockets – diaries hidden in socks – the
> sighs of a landscape covered in clothes –
> Alphabets disband in flocks spelling *stop*
> or *grace* or *mother*]

— I hoped you'd come back, she says

— *I am not sure for how long*

— That doesn't matter. Are you ready?

— *No*

> [This was not what they planned. It
> happened quickly. Suitcases bursting
> with invisible wealth. The voice susur-
> rant – *go now, leave, hurry* – voice housed

in the mind of a daughter carrying the
moon into midnight – her daughter too
– the pieces as if diamonds]

Dear Ghost

I

This letter is a texture in a language that neither of us really speaks. Although we do speak of small things so small that words relinquish their subject. We speak of air & dead people in newspapers. Today as I write the weather is unpredictable like a child on a beach searching for someone. I am uncertain of the accuracy of this image or any images in fact. A psychologist once said that a projection of two fantasies onto one another turns them into a childhood memory. I fantasise about a house with an apple tree & a kitchen large enough for us all. I fantasise about other people's families. Elsewhere he wrote the sentence, *various shades of meaning* & I think despite sounding like a cliché is rather delicate. But you are not interested in what a psychologist has to say, why should you be? Your silence is pronounced in our bodies, in how our hands reach for different belongings. Your fictions are yours to keep & mine to guess. What I am trying to say is something like sorry close to this meaning, which I always misinterpret, hide in its synonyms listening in this silence openly.

II

Slowly I unknot your fabrication like a reel of air in a spider's web.
        You flinch with discovery   & wince
    at the aerial contact of skin   &   the beautiful breath
                                of your meniscus body
you are a kernel of moonlight camouflaged in walls
& their crossings   dust of division & comfort.
Tenderly   I unbutton   so all that is left
        is the static shadow of light   before
& after   this movement.   I am twisted   &
apprehended
            in all these dark corners waiting
for our appearance   or   a memory   of what
            has never been.

III

Ghostly forms   mold migratory configurations
       intruder
foreign body   inhospitable guest
exotic   awkward   &   faraway
your skin is as pleasing   is as   cruel
as your tongue –   father of
           if only
      you could repeat yourself once more
show the inventory of this temporality
     in a glass vase of light
         & water
winter sunshine smoked with strangeness –
       this cold.

IV

uncertain   of
      a letter is a texture in a language   that
of skin   &   the beautiful breath of
  neither foreign body speaks   inhospitable
your meniscus body
elsewhere   he guest wrote the
skinless   a letter is a texture in a
sentence, various shades of skin is as pleasing   is
             language that neither of
all that is left of moonlight us really speaks
    winter sunshine smoked with
          you struggle to draft
  is the station bridge of lights strangeness
closely forms   mould migratory configurations

V

We are nature's apparitions

a sequence of sentences silhouetted

we ask   *what* does this mean?

we ask   *how* of our phrases?

letters   loose & loosening

                 letters

you struggle to draft   never shipped

a childhood   wanting

to hold one   between

fingers that rake   in this re-wilding

of language   & recall

to grow   in

                       our paper

                       thin bodies.

Family Values

You arrive at an exhibition called *Family Values*. It displays Zofia Rydet's monumental project, *Sociological Record* (1978-1990) comprising one thousand photographic portraits of individual Poles in their homes.

The house didn't exist. The father did not make contact. The mother did not speak much about the father or the house or who was left behind in the house. Until the house stood on her door step and knocked.

Not everything new and unfamiliar is frightening acknowledges the psychologist. In the same essay, he writes, *primitive fear of the dead is still so potent in us and ready to manifest itself if given any encouragement.* If only to be encouraged. You were encouraged to forget. You were encouraged not to ask.

At the exhibition Jozef Rabakowski's video installation films a lacework of neighbours and strangers. These cinematic figures, umbral and undecided move outside his kitchen window into their own lost homes.

A snow-clenched evening submissive to the lightness of a deepening hour. A girl runs from one block of flats to another calling for *mother* then disappears into the edges of recollection.

Until I was ready, until I was ready to come back, he answered, when you saw him for the first time.

Every woman in Rydet's photograph could be the grandmother and every room a cemetery, every wall, a headstone.

Reunited in memory, in conversation, in the writing of a photograph, in the actuality of being there as opposed to here.

Today is full of openings, contradictions and oversized apples pendent on small trees.

You repeat the phrase because you like the way it sounds and because in his difficult articulation, Derrida urges you to speak with ghosts, *Even if they are no longer, even if they are not yet.*

You travel from the airport to the village studying the trees in the orchards as if they were figures in a life drawing.

Her words are crooked doorways and you stoop to enter.

So many of us obsessed with houses, *One need not be a chamber to be haunted, One need not be a house,* she writes in her bedroom dressed in a white gown.

The ghosts are not talking but you hear them downstairs circulating in cold space, smoking cigarettes. They follow your father rattling in the haptic space of his mother.

A woman sells homegrown vegetables and fruit outside the cemetery. Earth in the traces of her hands and produce. Earth in the corner of *where* she stands and *where* she lives. Earth between you in language *where* it breaks.

Bachelard talks of words being little houses, *each with its cellar and garret.* You imagine language as the hut destroyed, and rebuilt on a wild island.

You buy two apples the size of a cat's skull. You buy plums too. You eat a whole bag of plums. You go back to buy more for your children and hope they will last the journey home.

The voice says, *I have spent my life growing up in the shadow of the peace line.*

You find words in streets and recycle them.

There are rooms in the shadows of previous rooms, houses unanswerable and doors seemingly open.

She filled it with cement and knocked down its walls. What remained was the negative space of a house.

In a story called, *Why Don't You Dance?* The protagonist empties his house of furniture and leaves it in the front yard. The inside free of possessions, the outside occupied by this space.

In another story, he pockets all of the possessions and leaves her crouching, dress unbuttoned, still damp.

Your father cooks soup and sausages with dumplings. Insists you drink coffee. Later you can't sleep and watch the branches handwriting their shapes on walls, which you have long ago demolished.

This is not a haunted house but you are haunted in it.

Unprepared, unexplained, un-thought, unforgiving, '*negative prefix un- is the indicator of repression*' says the psychologist. You arrive unannounced thirty years ago.

Part III

When all is said, what remains to be said is the disaster. Ruin of words, demise writing, faintless faintly murmuring: what remains without remains (the fragmentary).

—*Maurice Blanchot*

Winged Narratives

———

This morning the sky is *pastel* and flails in the symmetry of a flat landscape. *Pastel* from *past illus* or *pastellum* in Latin, meaning dough, small loaf, block. The sky is my grandmother's bread.

                                        Salted tomatoes on bread.

I eat the sky of this history.

———

March snow falls. We walk through pinewoods with our children. A waxen sea loops in parallel to this forest. The wind is relentless, holds all the power in its detachment and drill. Our son hides behind trees pretending he is a wolf. His howls unsettle the geography of spaces and speculation. In play, he changes from a wolf to a soldier, holding an improvised gun. He lurches. Pockets filled with pinecones. Throws them like grenades. Already embodied in war. Already confined in masculinity
– Already –

———

In the corner wall of a cellar, a spider constructs texts from years of hard labour.
There is vodka. Coal. There are old wardrobes. Patches of leather, sewing machines.

        A trumpet blowing the breeze of *him*.

The smell of black tea, fungi, the red of a bicycle escaping with its rider.

        And the woods carrying too many names in their bark.

———

Picture a ghost country in the middle of Europe.
Imperceptible shapes moving.
Stripped of language and body. Bloodied yet bloodless.
The ghost country stirs through centuries in a ghost haze.

The last lines of 'A Mirror for the Twentieth Century' reads:

A rock
Breathing with the lungs of a lunatic:
                    That is it
                    That is the Twentieth Century.

In a suitcased-city, a town is buried in its own streets
children curl, yellowing in the hands of snipers
                                        even the rain is dry.
A sunrise erased by the pummel of voices.

Gunfire un-stitches the sky
                    the bark of a dog in the distance
the whimper of a ghost as moths land on its shoulder.

————

In the woods, we find a dead hare. The carcass resembles a sculpture in an
exhibition, entitled, *Bodies and Boundaries*. Our son stares at the animal;
processing death not as fact but as narrative. The stillness of his questions
censored in sand and the pine needles at our feet.

————

In the Polish language *Dom*, meaning house is masculine as is the word
niezależność translated as independence. War, *Wojna* is feminine like,
historia and *percepcja*. But the word *oko* (the eye) is neuter. Could I be
impartial I ask myself?

————

Our daughter is practicing independence in the bathroom mirror.
Drawing the definition in her undisciplined skin. Tracing it in glass.

————

11th November 1918.

―――――

A colour is never seen as it really is. Colour deceives. For example, think red, Albers says. What red do I see? In its incalculable shades, red summons unaccountable readings.

What colour is independence?

―――――

I own a copy of a Polish map belonging to my grandmother. Łódź is shaded in the industrial spill of pewter. My grandmother's handwriting embroiders the edges with her expenditure: train tickets, vegetables, meat.

―――――

In 1971, Łódź was a city of women. In 1971, the women in the city of women remained in the factories, refusing to work. In 1971 they said, *Our kids eat black bread.*

―――――

There were 11 Jews living in Łódź in 1793, by 1897, nearly 99,000.
In different books and sources there are differing numbers.

In 1918, Łódź was one of the largest, industrious cities in Europe, living with one of the largest Jewish communities.

―――――

When I ask A. when her father came to Łódź, she cannot recall:
We never were into dates, she offers.

―――――

Nothing that has ever happened should be regarded as lost for history, Walter Benjamin writes.
To say that nothing is lost is to say that everything still exists.

―――――

Our daughter is learning how to separate herself from her childhood. I read about this process in a book and try to recall my own attempts of separation, this *losing what we have to say that we speak.*

———

Just before he went to prison, I found out I was pregnant, she tells me.

Apparently for stealing some leather or possessing a gun, or fighting for his country or being in the wrong place at the wrong time.

———

I have found new words for shades of red: amaranth, cinnabar,
                                        coquelicot, stammel.
Yet struggle with white.

———

A second childhood begins in a different country.

———

It is only a glass of water.
Water in a glass.
Glass holding water.
You are not allowed to offer the water.
But I am sure you want to.
You will be killed for offering the water.
Such were the rules in occupied Poland.

———

Documents of barbarism in cities with cobbled windows

boot prints erased on the earth's charcoaled maps

voices choked with hair

languages swept under the wingspan of other languages

translations of *what happened* pressing to be un-translated

skin mistaken for potato peelings

thumbs sucked until they are swallowed

———

How much clarity is possible in the meaning of *one* word?

———

Silver birches stand to attention, observant and silent. In witnessing, they grow taller as if unbroken by this damage, unchanged in air seized by bodies and forgetting.

———

Benjamin's *Angel of History* became Paul Klee's painting, *Angelus Novus*, a helpless angel stuck in a storm —

Wind marks the sky a violet-brown,
pigments the space with voices
from stretched mouths

groaning
in the rain-pour of invisibility.
The sky sucks its ink deeper.

Vertiginous swoops of sound,
the helplessness of air itself,
stick to the face of the angel.

She attempts to move her wings as if
to assemble the cruelty of the past.
She is paralyzed in her own sudden
inability to understand —

the tips of her wings crossed like fingers.

———

A friend buys me a book called *Museum of Angels, Guide to the Winged Creatures*. I am taken back to an orchard of oranges on a holiday twenty years ago and remember writing a poem called *Angels with Oranges*. I imagined the orchard as angels with distended bodies, winged narratives folding with affliction, my grandfather's history lucent and barbed.

We travel to Łódź. Walk along Piotrkowska Ulica, the longest street in Europe. The children eat páncki, jam spilling from the sugared dough. The afternoon is not fully inhabited either by people or by winter. The street is wide, renovated, sentenced. We carry *you* inside its complicated length.

In the same city in September 1939, trade in leather and textile goods are prohibited. Money is sewn into linings and the city sewn into ruined walls. Memory dangles in disguised gardens, flowers dissolve in the obscure shades of human hands.

If only she had awoken on time and met her soldier. If only she had taken his details. Fate fenced in our ground, that conditional space of our breathing.

In Łódź, we walk the phantom spaces of its boundaries, barriers, the survival of its air snagging on our footsteps. We hear the phantom blows and rumours of retreat. Patience thinning like people. We smell the phantom sweat and hopelessness of human skin. We tear each other open. Remove what is inevitable and not ours. Regain strength in separation.

Our woods are dewed, a damask of fallen bark and season. Our daughter in her distance hooks her childhood in clearings. Our son in her mirror and progress. Occasions are yet to unfold and we wait in its edges. A snow of sunlight settles on branches as we listen and *remember forgetfully: again, the outside.*